Praise for
Between Spiritual Highs

In his book *Between Spiritual Highs*, Sunny does a great job of helping Christians of all ages to maintain their spiritual highs. So often, Christians reach a spiritual high and then gradually make their way back to the "same old." But Sunny shows us biblical ways to not only maintain our spiritual highs, but to go beyond! Yes, we MUST go beyond! And Sunny (pointing to the Bible) shows us the way.

–**Joshua Kang**
Senior Pastor of Full Gospel Las Vegas Church

If you have ever been frustrated by riding a spiritual roller coaster I have good news for you. Sunny Kang has given us a helpful spiritual guide to getting off the roller coaster once and for all. This book is personal, practical, and powerful!

–**Dr. Dave Earley**
associate professor of Pastoral Leadership and Evangelism,
Liberty University School of Divinity

Author, Pastor Sunny Kang has spent his adult life working with and encouraging youth. He has a unique and practical perspective on Christian growth. This book focuses on seven principles of practical spiritual growth in the application of one of chief tools used in the Church for spiritual development for youth. The focus of *Between Spiritual Highs* is targeted at college and career age young adults. It is a refreshing lesson on application Christian growth principles to continue consistent Christian living between the mountain top experiences of special conferences, camps and retreats. Learning to live a consistent Christian testimony when one is alone is an important lesson in developing mature spiritual growth. I believe Pastor Kang has hit on a great formula for application of daily Christian living principles.

—Donald Cabbage
President of World Mission Society

I've been preaching around the world—56 countries to be more exact, and have witnessed many ups and downs of followers of Christ. This book, *Between Spiritual Highs*, is for those who want to grow in Christ with constant passion between retreats and revivals. This book will give you solid tools to apply between the spiritual highs and lows of your spiritual journey.

—Robert Oh
author of The Prayer Driven Life

Between Spiritual Highs will help church members and leaders navigate the roller coaster ride of short-term missions, retreats, and conferences; to harness the momentum from these experiences rather than billowing off of a cliff.

—Martin Malmberg
Director of Youth With A Mission Las Vegas

The church is filled with spiritual junkies who are continually chasing one high after another in retreats, conferences, and mission trips. Out of a holy discontent, Sunny unpacks practical teachings on how we can be a steadfast people, in his straight-forward, emphatic New York style.

—Christian Lee
Lead Pastor of New Philadelphia Church

I'm not a pastor or a missionary. I'm a college student, who grew up in Las Vegas. Pastor Sunny has been ministering to me for about ten years now and I can personally attest to the effectiveness of his teachings, as well as, his genuine desire to bless others. Reading this book made me realize that he has been teaching me these principles since I was in middle school. Even as we sit in cafés or hang out as a college group, these teachings keep coming back. It is possible to counter the highs and lows experienced around retreats and revivals. When practiced consistently, this book will help you go from glory to glory!

—BJ Kim
Youth Group and College Leader,
Full Gospel Las Vegas Church

BETWEEN SPIRITUAL HIGHS

Experience Breakthroughs Between
Retreats and Revivals

Sunny Kang

Unless otherwise indicated, Scripture quotations are from the ENGLISH STANDARD VERSION.

Copyright © 2001 by Crossway Bibles, a division of Good News Publishers.

All rights reserved. No part of this publication may be reproduced, distributed, or transmitted in any form or by any means, including photocopying, recording, or other electronic or mechanical methods, without the prior written permission of the publisher, except in the case of brief quotations embodied in reviews and certain other non-commercial uses permitted by copyright law.

This book is dedicated to my loving and faithful grandmother, Kyung Soon Kang. God has used you to protect me and grow me in unimaginable ways. All of your love, wisdom, and sacrifices are not wasted. Generations have already been blessed by you and many more will be blessed by you in years and years to come!

Table of Contents

Acknowledgements 11

Foreword 13

Introduction 15

Chapter 1 Communal Affirmation 19

Chapter 2 Biblical Affirmation 29

Chapter 3 Self-Affirmation 38

Chapter 4 Synergistic Prayer 50

Chapter 5 Faithful Obedience 58

Chapter 6 Sword Training 67

Chapter 7 Power of Your Testimony 76

Chapter 8 The Unveiling 86

Conclusion 95

Postscript 97

Appendix A 101

About the Author 109

Acknowledgements

There are many people to thank who have shown support in the publishing of this book. As always, it would be difficult to name every single person who helped somehow along the way. If my thanks began with all the family that have raised me, pastors that have discipled me, teachers that have taught me, and friends that have put up with me, this list would be bigger than the book itself!

This is just a short list of the many people who have been very encouraging at some point in this process of writing and publishing the book:

Full Gospel Las Vegas and FG West: Pastor Joshua Kang, Pastor Eun Kwang Ko, Pastor John Hong, Pastor Russell Greene, Marina Kang, Andrew Aguilar, BJ Kim, Sam Lee, Michael Finkle, Chung Oh, Junho Bae, Jenny Rice, Susanna Han, Laura Seo, Lisa Lee, Sueah Chung, and Jassica Kim.

SPS Community Members and Launch Team: Bonnie Dorough, Meredith Swift, Charlene Kugler, Leah Hill, Jill Rogers, Lisha Lender, Kelly Walk Hines, James Lamar, Henry Kim, Brett Cox, Jeannie Kang, Dustin Craft, Teresa Nelson, Esteban Salas, Sharon Kim, Paul Kwon, and Austin Jang.

The most involved in this process has been my lovely and amazing wife, Anna Kim Kang. Thank you Anna for just who you are and all that you do! Like I said on our wedding day, you are an unending treasure chest—I just get more and more amazed by you every day!

Thank you everyone (listed or not listed) who I have interacted with about this attempt at making a difference in the lives of many! Your support and contributions are appreciated much more than I can express!

A big thank-you to my editor, Spencer Borup, for his professional touch.

Foreword

This is the type of book that will truly help re-define your normal! As a traveling evangelist, I have personally seen the issue of "losing the fire" over and over in the lives of believers. I am so excited to see that there is a tool like this book to assist the body of Christ in overcoming this obstacle. Through tools like this, individuals and churches alike will have the ability to keep the fire going, internally converting from an "event" to a "lifestyle" of being in the presence of God. To get fed alone by your pastors or guest speakers is a very dangerous practice and, unfortunately, not discussed enough. I am ecstatic that Sunny has the courage a lot of individuals do not demonstrate, addressing hard topics like this to better the body. I have known Sunny for years and have seen the relentless approach he has to staying in the presence of God. He's always a student and always in prayer. He has become a true intercessor and a pure example of what it looks like to be a real "Christian."

We need more examples like this man in the church!

Through this book you will not only be given the teachings to understanding and accepting your true identity, but will be given tools on how to walk out a truly fire filled life.

I recommend this book to anyone looking to ignite their relationship with God and especially those who are struggling with keeping the fire ablaze between conferences!

Kevin Suter
International Evangelist & Minister
President of Catalyst Mobile
www.catalystmobile.org

Introduction

Have you ever come back from a Christian conference or a Christian retreat on fire for God and you somehow later became lukewarm? Do you recall experiencing indescribable blessings on a mission trip and eager to come home to change your church, only to find yourself doing nothing? Realistically, how long did it take for you to come back "down to earth"? Unfortunately, sometimes it gets worse than that. You may have seen friends experience these amazing blessings one week and tragically fall far from God soon after. Indeed, how tragic!

Here's the scary truth: *If we're not careful, we can all fall far from where we once were.* This pattern is nothing new. We could see the trend throughout the Bible, even evidenced in the church in Ephesus where Paul spent most of his time ministering (Revelation 2:5). Judging by the quality of the contents of Paul's epistles, there are indications that the most spiritual church in Asia Minor was that of Ephesus. They were on fire for a time, but lost much of it by the time Revelation was written.

The cyclical pattern of having spiritual highs followed by spiritual lows is a frustrating one. The secret to breaking this cycle has nothing to do with attending retreats, conferences, and mission trips. The key is what you do between these events in your everyday lives. After watching many people go through these cycles and experiencing these cycles myself, I conclude: no one likes such experiences.

This book, *Between Spiritual Highs*, was written to help you live above this trend. Christians need help as to growing between retreats, revivals, and mission trips, and maintaining their spiritual fervor as much as God desires for them. They need teachings and tools to apply between the spiritual highs of Christianity. If you acknowledge this tendency in yourself and want to do something about it, this book is for you.

As a pastor who has been to and led many retreats, having seen crowds of people "accept Christ," cry at the altar, and fall far from where they once were, I have identified at least seven teachings and practices for Christians to use between their "spiritual highs." In fact, I have used them myself to stay faithful between my own spiritual highs!

When Christians incorporate these practices in their lives, everything changes. With these practical, biblical, time-tested, and proven principles, you will have greater levels of joy, confidence, faith, and sense of purpose between retreats and revivals. And, your "default level" of Christianity will reach new levels! Your Christian life will be aglow with God's manifest presence. As Paul teaches, you reap what you sow (Galatians 6:7). So if you apply them to your life, you will reap the benefits.

Christians of all stages and backgrounds have applied these practices and have experienced new levels of faith. They've grown in new ways even within the first week of implementing these practices. Of course, those who practiced the applications in this book over a longer course have experienced even greater levels of growth.

Without doubts, life is too short to go through the same negative patterns and consequences. Before you know it, you may routinely go through life, experience another incredible spiritual high, and come back down to earth.

Wash.

Rinse.

Repeat.

Perhaps, that is okay for some. However, there are others who want more. This book is for those who want more.

My hope is that you would reshape the patterns of your spiritual life by applying the lessons in this book today. It is an honor to be a part of your spiritual journey!

Sunny Kang
College and Young Adult Pastor,
Full Gospel Las Vegas Church

Chapter 1
Communal Affirmation

"Death and life are in the power of the tongue, and those who love it will eat its fruits."
Proverbs 18:21

"Let no corrupting talk come out of your mouths, but only such as is good for building up, as fits the occasion, that it may give grace to those who hear."
Ephesians 4:29

Companies spend millions of dollars on advertisements with the sole goal of trying to expose our insecurities. When they succeed in getting us to feel insecure about ourselves, the greater the likelihood we buy their products. For instance, make-up ads make us feel "not so beautiful"; luxury car ads make us feel "not so luxurious"; vacation ads make us feel "not so satisfied" with the present. All these bombard our subconscious mind with thoughts until we begin to convince ourselves that the ads have judged us well.

But it's not only these paid advertisements that communicate our shortcomings, this culture has crept into our everyday relationships, as well. How many circles of friends practice "making fun of," "bashing," or "roasting" others? And how often do the same set of insults build, perpetuate, and get repeated again and again? Sure, we laugh it off and appear to be having a good time. But are we really?

If we're honest with ourselves, we would admit it's not always easy to shrug them off as mere fun. At some point, it seeps into our heads, our minds, and our souls. We start believing some of the direct or indirect criticisms about ourselves. This, then, adversely affects the way we live. I wonder how much of the garbage out there in the world has come into each of us. More importantly, what can we do about it when we are so immersed in such a culture?

I don't know about you, but I am so thankful for the Bible! God has the answer! In fact, the Bible gives us at least three answers to deal with the doubts, discouragements, and false self-ideologies that we have been told repeatedly. Once again, these toxic messages affect our thoughts and our behaviors. They even affect our relationship with God and others.

There are at least three ways to deal away with the lies that eat away at ourselves and our relationships. Due to the gravity of this problem, the first three chapters of this book is dedicated to first combat this attack. We will soon look into the first remedy, which is *Communal Affirmation*.

Before we delve into this concept of Communal Affirmation, we need to know what we should NOT do:

- Do not isolate yourself as though you were a hermit.
- Do not read the Bible only.

Isolating ourselves is not the answer because God made us for community. He made us for relationships. In Genesis 2:18, God says, "It is not good that the man should be alone." This scripture gives us an idea that certain things are not complete in themselves; they need complementary factors so they could bring forth a reasonable result. As controversial as it may sound, once upon a time, it was Adam and God; but, in His observation, God said it was NOT good. God and His Words alone were somehow not enough for Adam. He needed more. God has made people and created us for community. To combat the unhealthy garbage directed towards us, we actually need others.

The practice of "communal affirmation" is simply *intentionally receiving affirmations or encouragements from people in our community.* As spiritual garbage is communicated through people, spiritual cures are also communicated through people. As simple as it is to be affected by the shortcomings pointed out to us, we can also be affected by encouragements. The power of death is not only in the tongue, but so is the power of life (Proverbs 18:21).

At retreats, revivals, and on missions, people usually speak very kindly and are intentionally encouraging. To grow "between spiritual highs," we ought to carry this attitude over into our "real world." That is, good, positive, edifying words are not solely meant for spiritual environments like our prayer camps or retreats; we should learn to speak "grace" to one another in spite of the location. Believers must surround themselves with edifying and encouraging words everywhere.

In your normal surroundings, do you know what people around you value about you? Have you ever asked others to help identify your gifts, talents, and abilities? Do you know how much they value your unique contributions?

If not, you are missing out.

Hearing others speak about your good qualities and talents will do wonders! Of course, this is not saying you need other people's validation of who you are; we will explore this next chapter. The emphasis in this chapter is the importance of receiving encouraging words that will then encourage and motivate you to be who God truly called you to be.

If you understand the power of communal affirmation, you will help foster a community that will always believe the best for one another. People will celebrate each other's strengths. Even when someone demonstrates weakness, he or she will not be coldly criticized but encouraged to be who God called them to be.

Imagine this scenario: After teaching a class to teens, you felt you did your best but someone came saying you really messed it up. How would you feel? You would probably never want to speak again. Again, moments later, another fellow walked up to you, patted you on the back and said you did a great job and gave you examples of what really was impactful. This encouragement would help you to grow and develop your ministry. The former is damaging while the latter is healing.

Now, let's look at a case study on how this works.

Man of Encouragement

Myunghwa Choi was an intern pastor at New Philadelphia Church in South Korea. She spoke of an encouraging church leader named Brady Miller. To speak life into Pastor Myunghwa, he would often address her as "Princess Myunghwa!" "Princess Myunghwa, how are you today?" "Princess Myunghwa, you did a great job speaking today!"

Being on the receiving end, Pastor Myunghwa said she felt very awkward at first. She even felt like he was making fun of her. However, she shared as time went by and he kept calling her "Princess Myunghwa," and she would smile sometimes. Then she would entertain the thought a little. Sometimes she would even believe it. Little by little, she realized more of the truth according to God's Word. She realized how she is, in fact, God's daughter, or . . . a princess! Believing in who she is, according to the Bible, as spoken through a fellow believer, has done wonders for Pastor Myunghwa and for many others in her church.

What about me? After one Friday service, Brady, approached me. He said when he saw me walk into his church for the first time, he sensed the word "courage." Since then, he would often greet me saying, "Man of courage, how are you?" "Man of courage, good to see you!" "Hey, man of courage!" As Myunghwa experienced, I felt a little weird at first. Before long, however, I was "amen-ing" in my heart whenever he greeted me. I even started to straighten up my posture and walk with more confidence. I had doubts about myself sometimes, but I was regularly reminded by a brother in Christ who I really was: a man of courage. This book is just one evidence of the effect communal affirmation has had on me. (Thank you, Brady, man of encouragement!)

Encouragement Bank

The key is to hear encouragements and affirmations regularly. One time is not enough. We are forgetful people. We need to receive them and "deposit" them in our encouragement banks. We can then "withdraw" from them as needed.

As elementary as it may sound, I have writings and voice recordings saved on my phone of people's thoughts on my gifts, talents, character, and abilities. I turn to these again and again for encouragement. Why? Because so many unhealthy thoughts about myself tend to creep in sometimes. This is why I need to be intentional about what goes into my system.

Here are a few examples of what's in my encouragement bank:

"You're good."

My non-Christian (at the time, *anti*-Christian) father told me this after hearing me preach one Sunday. If my non-Christian father, who was not supportive of me being a pastor, could acknowledge my gift, I'm encouraged.

"Next to my parents, you have had the most influence on my life."

Junho Bae, a student wrote this in the form of a letter on two separate occasions. He wrote this to me once when he was in high school and once when he was in college.

"There's a lot of people who want revival, but are not willing to pay the cost. When I see you, I see a man who is willing to pay the cost."

Pastor Erin Lee from New Philadelphia Church said this to me years back and this strengthens me a great deal even today.

"We could tell you love your wife so much!"

Youth group and college students in my church have voiced this. This is encouraging because I REALLY do love my wife!

"I'm not worried about you. You'll do well."

Every three weeks, I get a haircut. I talk family, church, and life with my hair stylist, Valeria. In speaking of some uncertainties about future, she responded with this.

"Your character is unquestioned."

Pastor Eun Kwang Ko, the current Youth Pastor at my church shared this with me one time. We've known each other years before we became pastors.

"I've never heard a Korean preacher before today. I will remember your text and main points from today's message for the rest of my life."

A recovering addict told me this after guest speaking at his rehabilitation center.

"It's tough to find a church, but hearing you speak on Facebook is amazing. It felt like chasing the wind looking for a church . . . but now it feels like God found me. Please find the courage to keep doing it, as you have found the courage to start!"

A former church member looking for a church saw a Facebook Live message I attempted. I was discouraged, but she texted me these words. I continued to give short messages online every week. Currently, I am figuring out a better way to give these messages.

The above examples were from friends, family members, neighbors, strangers, Christians, and non-Christians. They encourage me so much! God can encourage through so many different people. With all of the garbage out there, I need to be intentional about what I keep in my system. Doing so has been a part of growing me to new levels and can have the same effect on you!

But what if people are not sincere or accurate? What if they are just off in their discernment of me? That is why we next turn to the second way to deal with doubts, discouragements, and false self-ideologies. But before turning the page, let's first make a difference in our lives today by practicing Communal Affirmation. Let's fill up your encouragement bank!

Put It to Practice!

1. In the past, can you remember key encouragements or affirmations you've received? They could be about your talents, abilities, or character. What were some of the best encouragements you've received and who were they from? Record them somewhere and refer to them often.

2. Can you email or text 5-10 friends? Sure, you can! Do it now! Say you're working on an assignment. Ask five friends or family members, "Can you tell me what you think my strengths, gifts, and talents are?" Feel free to share what you think their strengths, gifts, and talents are first. If you do this, replies will come back more quickly! And feel free to ask "Can you be more specific or give examples?" These will help you deposit more in your bank!

3. Can you actually approach three other people in your life this week and simply ask them the same question in person? Sure, you can! It can be people you work with, go to school with, or order food from! Again, feel free to say it is an assignment or that a church leader

recommends you make a list of "affirmations" from others. Chances are they will appreciate you approaching them, of all people. This should make for an edifying and encouraging conversation in person. And remember, when you share with them first, they will more easily share with you!

4. Would you like to take it up a notch? Of course, you do! Have a recording device like a phone ready and ask if you can record the other person sharing. It may feel weird for a moment, but this can turn out to be the best audio you have on your device. I made some of my recordings my alarm clock so I wake up to encouragement every single day!

If we're going to bring out the best in people, we too, need to sow seeds of encouragement.
Joel Osteen[1]

---

[1] Joel Osteen, *Become a Better You: 7 Keys to Improving Your Life Every Day*, Reprint edition (New York: Howard Books, 2009): 135.

Chapter 2
Biblical Affirmation

For you formed my inward parts; you knitted me together in my mother's womb. I praise you, for I am fearfully and wonderfully made.

Psalm 139:13-14a

All Scripture is breathed out by God and profitable for teaching, for reproof, for correction, and for training in righteousness.

2 Timothy 3:16

In the previous chapter, we looked at the importance of community and the words they speak. It is worth reiterating how men and women were created for relationships. Once again, God said in Genesis 2:18, *"It is not good that the man should be alone."* However, please do not misunderstand; this is not saying God was not enough for man, concerning salvation. In terms of living out our faith, He is a God of relationships. He designed us for community. As some of you may have guessed, in this chapter, we will turn to how God and His Words are also essential to growing between spiritual highs.

God vs. Man

The limitations of people include men and women being fallible. People's encouragements can take us a long way.

When we fill our encouragement banks with affirmations from various people, we protect our views of self. However, nothing is quite as authoritative as God and His Word.

God, on the other hand, has authority over us because, first and foremost, He created us! In Psalm 139:13, we learn how He even created us in our mother's womb. As Creator over all things, He has the authority to speak into our lives as no one else can. When man's opinions and God's Word conflict, God's Word is true every single time! When my thoughts and God's Word about myself conflict, God's Word is true every single time!

God's Word in Churches

God's Word is essential to a Christian's growth. Many churches do well to teach Bible stories from Genesis to Revelation. Most people who grew up in church can tell you about Adam, Noah, Joseph, David, Deborah, Elijah, and the Apostles. They may also be able to tell you a handful of parables Jesus taught. These stories tell us much about God and His dealings with man and are very important.

People who grew up in churches should also be able to list many *Do*'s and *Don't*s of the Bible. They may be able to list most of the Ten Commandments, talk about spiritual disciplines and doctrines, and recite the Lord's Prayer in more than one version.

What may surprise people who grew up in the church, however, is how God thinks of them. What may need to be emphasized more in churches is how God thinks of us, who He created us to be, and what He thinks of me at this very moment. How has God designed us and who has He called us to be? Your answers to these questions are only as powerful as aligned with God's Word.

Our churches must change gears and begin to teach people how they ought to see themselves from God's viewpoint. It's not enough to share those Bible stories and doctrines (which sometimes are denominationally biased), it's important to see ourselves the way God sees us. The first step to this is seeing the Bible as the highest and truest authority over our lives.

Biblical Encouragement Bank

This next section will highlight twelve biblical truths about myself, which I have stored in my Biblical Encouragement Bank. I turn to them often because they are spiritually and emotionally rich! If you pay close attention, you may see a progression. And by the way, these truths are for you too!

1. So God created man in his own image, in the image of God he created him; male and female he created them. – Genesis 1:27

"I am made in the image of God!" When God created me, He figuratively looked in the mirror or at Jesus and created me! I am not a rip-off, I'm the real thing! I have some of the qualities of God!

2. For God so loved the world, that he gave his one and only Son, that whoever believes in him should not perish but have eternal life. —John 3:16

"I am loved!" The apostle John identified himself as the one "whom Jesus loved" (John 13:23) and we can too! God loves us with an unconditional love. Before Jesus performed one miracle, saved one soul, preached one sermon, God communicated His love for Jesus (Matthew 3:17). However we feel about ourselves, the truth is, God loves us unconditionally!

3. For Christ Jesus you are all sons of God, through faith. —Galatians 3:26

"I am a child of God!" I am God's son (or daughter) because I have truly placed my trust in Him. I have been adopted into His family! I receive family benefits, including a direct line to Him!

4. And if children, then heirs—heirs of God and fellow heirs with Christ, provided we suffer with him in order that we may also be glorified with him. —Romans 8:17

"I am heavenly royalty!" I am not just loved by God, I am royalty! As a child of God and co-heir with Christ, I am a prince (or princess) in His kingdom! According to some translations, I am a king (Revelation 1:6, 5:10). The point is, royalty lives according to another standard. They carry themselves differently. I am royalty!

5. For I know the plans I have for you, declares the Lord, plans for welfare and not for evil, to give you a future and a hope. —Jeremiah 29:11

"God has great plans for me!" Though there will be times life will not go my way, God has great plans for me! Though there will be difficult times, God has great plans for me! I can live each day knowing God has great plans for me.

6. As each has received a gift, use it to serve one another, as good stewards of God's varied grace. —1 Peter 4:10

"I am gifted!" Because this one is harder for me to believe, I repeat three times: "I am gifted!" "I am gifted!" "I am gifted!" God has given me at least one gift to be effective. I am gifted to serve others and help them along their journey through life.

7. For we are [God's] workmanship, created in Christ Jesus for good works, which God prepared beforehand, that we should walk in them. —Ephesians 2:10

"There's a job only I can do!" God created me like a certain key to unlock certain locks. He created the lock and the key. He created me and the good works I am to do beforehand. There are some things only I can do. I am designed, shaped, and prepared to influence specific people in ways that no one else can.

8. You are the salt of the earth, but if the salt has lost its taste, how shall its saltiness be restored? —Matthew 5:13a

"I am made to mingle with others!" I am made to make contact. I am not called to be isolated and distant from others. I bless others by intentionally rubbing shoulders with them.

9. You are the light of the world. A city set on a hill cannot be hidden. —Matthew 5:14

"I am seen by others and that is great!" The reason is, I shine God's light with good deeds. As I follow Christ, people see what Christ looks like through my life.

10. Now you are the body of Christ and individually members of it. —1 Corinthians 12:27

"I am made to be part of a body." I am not made to be a loner. I am made to grow with a community of believers with different backgrounds and gifts. Through the body, I can grow and help others grow.

11. For those whom [God] foreknew he also predestined to be conformed to the image of his Son, in order that he might be the firstborn among many brothers. —Romans 8:29

"I will have many brothers and sisters to bless!" God created me in His image and to be the "firstborn" among many. I will have many to bless, care for, and disciple.

12. Truly, truly, I say to you, whoever believes in me will also do the works that I do; and greater works than these will he do, because I am going to the Father. —John 14:12

"I will do greater things than Jesus!" This can mean the local church or global church I am a part of, or it can mean myself. Either way, this is not a small statement by Jesus. I will do greater things or the body of Christ which I am a part of will do greater things than Jesus did while on earth. This is according to God's Word!

Limitations of Knowledge

If you did not "Amen!" to any of those verses, why not? Read them again and make them yours! If you did "Amen!" in your heart, there is still need for caution.

Imagine a drug in the form of a pill that can cure discouragement, doubt, and false self-ideologies. Now imagine you swallow it, but the capsule is so hard it doesn't dissolve. Will you be cured? Unfortunately, no!

The Word of God is the cure. Many people "take in" the cure, which is God's Word, but they only have knowledge from God's Word in their heads. However, the "capsule" only dissolves when we believe His Word. It is not good enough to agree in our heads. The Word needs to be believed from the depths of our hearts. Biblical agreement must happen in the heart; then and only then does it take effect in our lives.

How would you know you truly believe the Word with your heart and not your head? One way to tell is even if circumstances and people's opinions are saying the opposite of the Word, you won't be moved because God's Word is an "anchor" to your soul (Hebrews 6:19). More so, you demonstrate belief in the Word when you walk it, live it, act it, think it, and speak it. It will affect your emotions, attitude, and outlook. On the other hand, if you allow false ideologies of self and discouragement to remain, you may not believe God's Word as much as you think. Once again, do you truly believe in God's Word, even over your own?

You've taken a glimpse into my Biblical Encouragement Bank. Now it's time to make deposits into yours.

Put It to Practice!

Here are a few suggestions to practice right now:

1. Take those Bible verses listed above and rewrite them on a separate paper or electronic device.
2. Meditate on those verses one by one and now write your own summary or reflection on each verse like I did above. Take your time. Marinating is far better than microwaving! What does the verse(s) say about you?
3. As you read the Bible, listen to sermons, and read books, store up Bible verses that affirm who you are according to God. The references in this chapter are great, but not enough! We need more of the Word of God.

4. Over the next few days, try repeating the above process with the following verses:
   a. Psalm 23:1-6
   b. Joel 2:25
   c. Matthew 4:19
   d. John 15:5
   e. Romans 8:37
   f. 2 Corinthians 5:17
   g. Galatians 2:20
   h. Philippians 4:4-6
   i. Hebrews 3:13
   j. Revelation 19:9

Communal affirmation and biblical affirmation are not enough to grow you in your everyday life! Practice biblical affirmation for some time before moving on to the next chapter, which is the third key to growing between spiritual highs.

> *The Bible was not given for our information but for our transformation.*
>
> **D.L. Moody**[2]

---

[2] Bruce Wilkinson, The Seven Laws of the Learner: How to Teach Almost Anything to Practically Anyone, (Colorado Springs, CO: Multnomah Books, 2005): 146.

Chapter 3
Self-Affirmation

Why are you down, O my soul, and why are you in turmoil within me? Hope in God; for I shall again praise him, my salvation.

Psalm 42:5

One of his disciples, whom Jesus loved, was reclining at table at Jesus' side.

John 13:23

The One You Talk to Most

Have you ever been in a place where no encouragement or Bible verse was helping? What do you do then? When I was going through a rough patch in my ministry and personal life, no encouragement or Bible verse was sufficient to get me out or give me perspective. In my case, I got the crazy idea to preach my way out of it. I sat down and wrote down what I thought was happening and attempted to pick myself up. Below is what I wrote. Keep in mind, it was a rough patch and when you go through rough patches, you may sound a bit different.

Here it is:

01/26/2014

I am an ARROW. God is sharpening me to go FIRST and FORWARD and FURTHER than ANYONE has ever gone before—in my metron.[3] *God is preparing me for the RIGHT TIME to INCREASE and FURTHER my territory. Better yet, OUR [my church's] territory. The pains and frustrations all add up to MOLDING me and MENDING me and SHARPENING ME to be FIT for greater works.*

This requires RESOLUTE commitment to a process—God's process. God will use EVERYTHING He wants to make me SHARPER, STRONGER, SUAVER, and STEADIER! He will use LEADERSHIP, [YOUTH GROUP], FAMILY, FRIENDS, STRANGERS, PEOPLE FROM THE PAST, to accomplish His purpose IN me. He will use intentional events and supposed "accidents" to fulfill all of the above IN me. He will use "good events" AND "bad events" to prepare me for the GREATEST events of my life.

It is a SET UP!

God is pulling the strings and HE WILL ACCOMPLISH HIS PERFECT PURPOSES IN ME!

I am an ARROW. God has thrust me into the fire because it is right about time. He is SHARPENING ME to go FIRST and FORWARD and FURTHER than ANYONE has ever gone before—in my metron. God is preparing me for the RIGHT TIME to INCREASE and FURTHER my

---

[3] "Metron," here, refers to one's spiritual territory God has given the person responsibility over.

territory. Better yet, OUR territory. The pains and frustrations all add up to MOLDING me and MENDING me and SHARPENING ME to be FIT for greater works.

So BE BOLD and COURAGEOUS for the LORD OUR GOD IS WITH US!

BE CONFIDENT AND PATIENT. BE LOVING AND KIND. FOR AT THE PROPER TIME, YOU WILL SEE INCREASE! AT THE PROPER TIME, YOU WILL REAP A HARVEST!

THOSE WHO SOW IN TEARS WILL REAP A HARVEST WITH JOY!

MAY YOUR SOWING TEARS OF SORROW TURN TO HOPE-FILLED TEARS OF JOY!

BECAUSE IF YOU SEE WHAT GOD SEES, THERE IS NO ROOM TO STAY ANGRY OR FRUSTRATED AND MOST DEFINITELY NOT DISCOURAGED!!

GOD IS JOYFUL THIS VERY MOMENT FOR YOU!

WHY? BECAUSE THIS IS THE FURTHEST YOU HAVE EVER COME AND YOU ARE ONLY GETTING CLOSER AND CLOSER TO IMMEASURABLE AND UNREALISTIC INCREASE!

SO PUT YOUR HEAD UP AND GIVE GLORY TO YOUR FATHER IN HEAVEN THIS DAY!

AMEN!

Self-Talk

Sometimes, it is not enough to hear from others or even to read the Bible. King David was once in a tough situation and he had no one to strengthen him with soothing words. So what did he do? *He encouraged himself,* meaning, he talked some sense into himself that he could make it with God's help; and he made it. I did the same—as seen in my note above—and it infused courage to my downcast soul.

It's true that people are influenced by what others say, which is why communal affirmation is so effective. The Bible is certainly in a league of its own, especially in terms of power, which is why biblical affirmation is greatly effective. However, without negating the previous two, self-talk is also highly powerful and effective. In fact, when people cannot counsel or encourage themselves in their own words, the power of the previous two may even be negated. If you observed it, you would agree that my self-talk has its root in God's Word, which is key. It was a way of re-echoing divine truths written about me. Self-talk, emphasized in this book, is therefore expressing agreement with the Word in your own words and life.

The importance of encouraging self cannot be understated. Countless people in society—athletes, performers, public speakers, and more—usually ready themselves before big moments by talking to themselves. Say it out loud; it has therapeutic effect on your mental preparedness for the next pursuit or line of action—your morale is enhanced. It's empowering and healing when you talk to your *self*, using God's truths.

On the other hand, if our self-talk is harsh, we can cripple ourselves. Imagine what would happen to a child calling herself "fat" and "ugly" every time she looked in the mirror; or if a boy kept repeating "I suck!" after missing the mark in a sport. If our self-talk is condemning, the fruit will show through being angry, sad, or even becoming depressed. The power of death is certainly in the tongue (Proverbs 18:21).

For this reason, you employ the life-giving power of your tongue to move your life forward agreeing with God and His Word. If our self-talk is biblically uplifting, it can do wonders. Encouraging self-talk can be the difference between quitting and succeeding. Self-affirmation can be the difference maker at your next interview, difficult meeting, or stormy season.

Self-Talk in 3 Bible Characters

For David, encouraging self was the difference between depression and joy. He was clearly "cast down" and "in turmoil" (Psalm 42:5). However, after preaching to himself, he knew where he had to put his trust. He told himself, "Hope in God . . ." and decided to "praise him" (v5).

For the Apostle John, he decided to identify himself as the disciple "whom Jesus loved" (John 13:23). Even though

Jesus nicknamed him and his brother "Sons of Thunder" (Mark 3:17), John chose to self-identify differently.

Elsewhere in Jesus' time, one woman was suffering for twelve years. She had a bleeding problem, probably related to menstrual bleeding (Matthew 9:20). While Jesus was traveling and highly requested to perform miracles, this woman mustered up the confidence to approach him. According to Matthew, "for she said to herself, 'If I only touch his garment, I will be made well' " (Matthew 9:21). She followed through and got her blessing (v22).

What wonders encouraging self-talk can do!

3 Types of Self-Affirmation

What are ways you talk to yourself? Do you talk down on yourself? Do you highlight what you're not good at often? Do you give yourself limits that do not come from God? This could be the difference maker in your life! Put away harmful and hindering self-talk and replace them with truth!

There are different ways to talk to yourself, as seen in the above examples.

Emotional Breakthrough

First off, we can be like David and point ourselves to God when our thoughts or heart are not in the right place.

For example, if your thoughts were constantly negative, you can tell yourself:

"Christian, God is over all of this in some way, shape, or form. Trust Him!"

"Why are you constantly unhappy, David? God has something good up His sleeve, as always!"

"Jamie, God is willing and able to transform your thoughts. Go to Him!"

Self-Identification

Secondly, we can be like John and talk to ourselves about our identities. After all, if doing flows from being, we need to be clear about the "being" part.

When you face doubts about your worth or value among certain people, you can say the following statements:

"I am loved and valued by God no matter what anyone says."

"I am a valuable part of God's team."

"You can't make everyone happy. But make sure you're representing God well!"

Spiritual/Physical Breakthrough

Lastly, we can be like the woman with the medical problems of twelve years and preach ourselves into doing something that may be scary.

Let's say you are afraid of having a difficult talk with someone causing trouble, you can say the following to yourself in your own words:

"If I don't make this approach, this person may repeat the same behavior and cause even more problems."

"If I do make this approach in love, ultimate, long-term good will come from it."

Now, like the previous chapters, this may sound basic and elementary. However, when you sit down and get ready to give yourself a "real talk," you may even surprise yourself.

What Others Cannot Do For You

Let's reiterate this fact that even though other people's encouraging comments are necessary for you, in your journey, you will need more. While others and the Bible can say some truly helpful truths, they cannot communicate certain details that only you can communicate.

As you are the one going through something, you have a viewpoint on what is happening that no one else has. This is where you have a unique credibility. Being on the "receiving" end, you are able to observe what God is doing in your own, unique way.

When I was going through a rough time in early 2014, there was no one and no Bible verse that was able to get me through that storm; I felt stuck as if everything was blank.

The encouragement bank on my phone and the Biblical encouragement bank helped, but were not enough. I needed to increase my faith by proclaiming what I truly felt God was doing. Some things cannot be counseled away, they need to be proclaimed.

I needed to "dig deep" and speak to my soul in a way no one else could.

And so I did.

Without contradicting the Bible and without putting anyone down, I truly spoke out what I thought was happening and brought my attention back to the God over my life.

As I read and re-read what I wrote, I believed it more and more. Before long, the clouds of confusion and discontentment began to disappear. I was surprised by the level of authority in my tone. Re-reading what I wrote back then even ministers to me today!

Sometimes you have to preach, encourage, and motivate yourself to new levels.

A More Recent Example

To be honest, I am not going through the easiest time these days either.

Here is an attempt to practice what I preach today (03/30/2017):

Sunny,

You have no reason to be down (for long) because He is up! God is up to some good, actually LOT'S of good! Like the donkey holding back Balaam because of the fiery angel, sometimes you are held back from going someplace—for your own good-praise God!

Like David who was not forgotten when Samuel came to Jesse's house, you are not forgotten!

Like Elijah, whose brook ran dry, you have NOTHING to worry about!

You have the ability to show supernatural peace through your current storm.

As you show peace and confidence through this storm, God's hand will become more evident in your life.

Amen.

It is certainly different writing to myself knowing this will be read by people. However, it was still powerful and resonated enough for me to "get back on track." Some will call this "inspiration" or receiving a *rhema* of Scripture—taking biblical truths and applying it to specific, personal circumstances. Self-talk can be quite powerful!

Tips to Keep in Mind

Here are tips as you preach to yourself:

1. Acknowledge how you're feeling—directly or indirectly.
2. Be consistent with the Bible.
3. Keep in mind your maturing process of becoming more like Christ, which is called "sanctification."
4. Have a high view of God, which includes His unconditional love for you, good plans for you, and perfect timing.
5. Speak with confidence!

Put It to Practice!

Are you going through a difficult or dry time? Speak to yourself! You have the power of life in your tongue! What do you believe God is doing? Without contradicting the Bible, what do you feel is really going on in your life?

Practice speaking into your identity. What negative, unbiblical thoughts do you have about yourself? Counter them with the Word of God in your own words!

Is there something you have been putting off for a while? Speak to yourself! What will happen when you do what you need to do? Who will be impacted? What will happen if you don't do it? Perhaps you can use verses from the previous chapter to speak into your own life!

Resolved, never to do anything, which I should be afraid to do, if it were the last hour of my life.
Jonathan Edwards[4]

---

[4] Jonathan Edwards "The Resolutions of Jonathan Edwards" http://www.apuritansmind.com/the-christian-walk/jonathan-edwards-resolutions/ (Accessed May 9, 2017).

Chapter 4
Synergistic Prayer

Then [Jesus] said to them, "My soul is very sorrowful, even to death; remain here, and watch [pray] with me."

Matthew 26:38

Brothers, pray for us.

1 Thessalonians 5:25

Therefore, confess your sins to one another and pray for one another, that you may be healed.

James 5:16a

I had the amazing privilege of teaching at a Christian school for four and a half years. Like all teachers can relate, some days were easier than others. One particular day, the class I was teaching was especially difficult for me. Before long, I either blew up or was about to blow up. I do not remember exactly. What I do remember was walking out of the classroom, with a bewildered mind. On getting to the next floor, I found a teacher friend teaching his class. I signaled through the window for him to come outside for a moment to talk. This is how the conversation went:

Me: I almost had it with my class.
Friend: Oh really? What happened?
Me: They're just rowdier than usual and I almost lost it.

Friend: Sorry man. What can I do for you?
Me: Can you pray for me?
Friend: Sure, I can do that.
Me: Now
Friend: Now?
Me: Yes
Friend: Uh . . . sure.

My friend then prayed for me on the spot outside of his classroom. Perhaps a few people passed by or looked back. It didn't matter. I needed prayer and I got it. That prayer was a combination of encouragement, strength, support, and teamwork.

Have you had people casually share their prayer requests with you?

Did you always pray for their requests?

Me neither! (Sorry, friends and church members reading this book!)

Praying with others can have different forms.

The form highlighted in this chapter is actually praying out loud for a friend or neighbor like my friend did for me.

Jesus' Example

During the most difficult stretch of Jesus' life, He prayed. He often prayed in a place called Gethsemane with His disciples. On the night He was betrayed, He prayed asking

God if it were possible to take the burden of the cross away from Him (Matthew 26:39, 42). He was in incredibly deep anguish and He requested for His disciples to pray with Him. If Jesus, the greatest being of all, requested for imperfect people to pray with Him, who are we to think otherwise?

On this particular occasion, He was not worried about making others feel uncomfortable. He actually woke them up because He needed people to pray with Him. If we are to grow in our everyday lives, there needs to be room for praying for and with others.

Benefits of Synergistic Prayer

Ecclesiastes 4:9-10 says, *"Two are better than one, because they have a good reward for their toil: For if they fall, one will lift up his fellow. But woe to him who is alone when he falls and has not another to lift him up!"* Everyone reading this book probably agrees praying is essential to the Christian life. They may also agree how effective it can be to pray for others. However, how many of our lives reflect us actually taking advantage of this powerful weapon of synergistic prayer? Perhaps listing a few benefits will help us move from "just knowing" to action.

1. *Special Grace.* As we saw earlier in Biblical Affirmation, Ephesian 2:10 says there is a particular work only I can do. There is a contribution only I can make. The same is true for others. When others pray for people, they add something only they can contribute! What they

pray for may include requests you may not have considered. Not only does God work through people's encouragements, as we've seen in Communal Affirmation, God also works through people's prayers. In fact, some affirmation and encouragement can come as people pray for others.So we need to practice praying with others out loud!

2. *Protection.* Paul tells us in Ephesians 6:16, 18 to "take up the shield of faith" and to pray "at all times in the Spirit, with all prayer and supplication." Soldiers back then used shields to cover each other side by side making a huge barricade against all arrows and darts. One way Christians protect each other is by praying side by side so the enemy does not get in any of his deadly arrows. Are we engaging in this battle side by side with anyone? We need to!

3. *Edification.* Sharing topics and concerns can lead to a time of helpful counsel. There can be power in the prayer and there can be power in the counsel that follows. We can truly edify people in more ways than one when we not only say we will pray for them, but actually do.

4. *Honor.* When we turn to others for prayer, we honor them. We communicate, "I believe in your prayers," "I need your prayers," and "I value your faith and believe you can help me get through this." The reverse is also true. When someone allows me to pray for them, I am

honored to be trusted and to be a part of their spiritual growth.

Methods of Synergistic Prayer

1. *Approach and ask.* This is what I did to my school friend. I approached and I asked. I've done this countless times. Sometime ago, after a church meeting, I asked my pastor friend to have a talk with me for a few minutes. I shared with him what really bothered me and asked him to pray for me then and there. It wasn't the first time I asked him and, therefore, it wasn't the first time I benefited!

2. *Call and ask.* Praying over the phone can feel really awkward. However, I have done this when I could not approach anyone physically. Whether it was late at night or running around, at times, I needed prayer from a pastor or friend and received it through the phone. Depending on the gravity of the situation, it helped tremendously!

3. *Video chat and ask.* I have not tried this one yet, however, I'm sure it will also work. The point is, God is pleased when He sees His children encouraging one another and turning to Him for grace.

Tips When Asking

1. Every believer is capable of making an impact. Feel free to approach people that are not pastors. Pastors love praying for people; however, they are not meant to be

the only ones praying for others. Approaching others can give them confidence and a chance to grow in this intercessory area.

2. Be careful how much you share. Every believer is capable of praying for you. However, some information is more sensitive than others. Sharing more intimately should be done with people you trust more and who have demonstrated a certain level of maturity.

3. Most churches would feel comfortable keeping these one-on-one approaches same gender. Spiritual encouragement can lead to confusing relational lines between opposite genders. If you want to pray for people of the opposite gender or vice versa, perhaps praying with three or more people would be better. Guard your testimony. When in doubt, double-check with a leader of your church for accountability.

4. After the person prays for you, feel free to ask, "Did you get anything while praying for me?" This may be new to some people. It may also sound a bit risky. What if they say something unbiblical? Actually, all words need to be discerned. This goes for communal affirmation and counsel. After praying with someone one time, I asked if he "got anything" while praying for me. He shared, "As I was praying for you, I felt that you should stay faithful where you are and not force anything. God will lead you. So I don't think you should be forcing anything right now." This was

biblical and pertinent to my current situation. In discerning, it also helps to consider the maturity of the believer.

Put It to Practice!

Growing between "spiritual highs" involves a lifestyle change. Many retreats and mission trips involve people praying for each other. The benefits of this practice is not limited to Christian retreats. This is to be practiced regularly throughout our Christian lives.

1. The next time you need prayer, approach someone and ask them to pray for you. Being discerning of the environment, ask them to pray for you on the spot. It can stretch both of you!

2. The next time someone asks you for prayer, suggest praying for him or her on the spot. Again, it may feel awkward, however it will be worth it.

3. After praying for someone or being prayed for, feel free to talk about anything that was "gotten" or "sensed" while praying. As long as it does not contradict the Bible and discernment is used, God can greatly use these impressions to bless you.

4. It helps to ask your pastor or church leader you have a relationship with, in advance, if he or she welcomes prayer over the phone when needed. Most likely, he or she will be very happy to pray for you. We pastors love praying for people!

What we cannot obtain by solitary prayer we may by social. How so? Because where our individual strength fails, there union and concord are effectual.

John Chrysostom[5]

---

[5] Duewel, Wesley L., Mighty Prevailing Prayer: Experiencing the Power of Answered Prayer, (Grand Rapids, MI: Zondervan, 2013), 124.

Chapter 5
Faithful Obedience

Jesus said to them, "My food is to do the will of him who sent me and to accomplish his work."
John 4:34

If you love me, you will keep my commands . . . Whoever does not love me does not keep my words.
John 14:15, 24a

So also faith by itself, if it does not have works, is dead.
James 2:17

Have you ever had a hobby you were interested enough in to read about on your own? I did not grow up enjoying reading. However, I noticed when I was really interested in something, somehow I was able to read on that topic.

Growing up, I enjoyed the game of chess. I enjoyed it enough to read about it. (Yes, there are books on chess.) Later with the Internet, I was able to access databases of games from chess masters from decades ago. My favorite chess player was Bobby Fischer. While away from the game, he's had his issues, but he was quite the chess prodigy. Sometimes I found myself just watching his games move by move. I noticed especially how he would open. For reasons I couldn't tell, he would move this pawn here and tuck his bishop away there. I do know one thing for certain: as I played others and thought to myself "What would Bobby Fischer do?" I found my chess rating go up!

Something similar happens when we read the Bible, observe faithful men of the past and emulate them, especially Jesus! Though we may not know all the reasons why a certain practice is helpful, we are better off doing it for sure.

"Obedience" is not one of the words people get excited about. After all, it sounds like a word we want children or even dogs to grasp, but not ourselves. Though I never owned a pet or had a child (yet), I'm pretty sure parents and pet owners have the best interest in mind when wanting to be listened to.

As parents know and love their children more than children realize, God loves and knows us infinitely more than we can imagine. He is worth trusting and obeying!

Objections to Faithful Obedience

Before going any further on the topic, we should first acknowledge why it is so difficult to obey at times.

There are a few common obstacles to faithful obedience that need to be addressed.

1. *Lack of understanding.* People think because they do not understand something, it is difficult to follow.

True, understanding is helpful. However, observe how any successful movie director gives people on set their roles, responsibilities, lines, and deadlines for the good of the whole. Similarly, God does the same for us. We may not understand everything at the moment, however one day we will see how it all comes together. On that day, we will not regret faithfully following Him!

2. *Fear of rejection.* Some of what God calls us to do involves reaching out to others.

   The truth is when we reach out to others, whether to evangelize, reconcile, confront, counsel, or encourage, we may be rejected. Everyone understands the fear of rejection as our self-worth can be questioned.

   Believe it or not, rejection has its benefits. For one, we can relate more to He who was rejected more than any other man. Secondly, showing God's love after being rejected magnifies His love through you. The world pays attention to love that doesn't make sense. Though people's hearts may be hard, God's love is about to be magnified through you!

3. *Fear of missing the mark.* Fear of rejection has to do with people, but fear of missing the mark is fear of doing the wrong thing.

   Have you ever thought God wanted you to do something, but were not 100 percent sure it was Him?

What do you do when there isn't a burning bush or a fleece test available? This fear has hindered many from growing. A quick test on whether it was God or not is as simple as double checking with the Bible. If something contradicts the Word, hold it right there! If you are not sure if it is in the Bible or not, check with a mature Christian (or multiple Christians). God has given us the Word and community to protect us.

Here is one comfort, God is greater than our mistakes. Many times, professional athletes run plays and sometimes "misread" the signs from their teammates or coaches. God is greater than those teammates or coaches. He can take it if you were sincerely wrong and draw up another play.

Though Christians sometimes "score baskets" for the other team, our God is the greatest coach! His overall plan is not thwarted (Proverbs 21:30)! He will partner with us to make course corrections. So if you get that hunch to call someone or get the feeling you should give that huge check to a struggling church member, it's okay to be wrong. Go for it!

A Personal Testimony

My understanding of being an obedient Christian was primarily about reading the Bible. I noticed many Christians who were not diligent in the Word. In fact, I knew of Christians of ten, twenty, thirty years who never read the Bible once. As a result, I vowed to read diligently.

One year, I read the Bible three times in six months. The scary thing is, I did not gain much the second or third time around. It was then I thought I needed to go to seminary. Before that, however, I decided to do something I haven't really done before. I decided to give evangelism a try.

I was so afraid of evangelizing in an evangelism class offered at church, I skipped out on cold witnessing with the teaching pastor. It was required for everyone taking the class, but I could not and did not do it.

After reading the Bible three times in six months, I decided to finally give it a shot. There was an added problem this time. I was teaching in Korea and Korean was not my native language. I was not fluent, but somewhat conversational. In my quest of trying to be obedient, for thirty days, I vowed to hand out at least three evangelism tracts a day and have one conversation with a stranger.

It was scary . . . but awesome! I usually approached people who were smoking or just sitting around a nearby subway station. Most were willing to have a simple conversation, some were not interested. I found myself having thoughts about Christianity that I've never considered. Here are a few things I've learned:

1. A taxi driver didn't go to church because he had no money. I said people don't really look at that at church. He said they do. I began to believe him and felt sad about the church.

2. Mr. Kwak asked me how to get something off of the earth. What? I said by launching it off with a rocket. He said I was right. If the earth were covered with water from Noah's flood, where did all the water go? The water cycle says basically all the water is on a repeating cycle. I was dumbfounded. It made me study more.

3. A homeless woman was bitter and angry about how people messed up her life. She was very loud and others were watching us as we conversed. I found myself getting frustrated and got loud back. I told her she must have done something wrong too, but she's not telling me any of that part. She got quiet. I don't think evangelism books ever teach to yell back at someone, but it worked for us. We would be on good terms while I was in Korea.

4. I learned a bit of what Jesus did in the gospels! I was able to identify with Jesus more! As He walked the streets and had conversations with people He just met, I was doing something similar. On top of that, my prayer life changed and the Bible I did not get anything out of days before, opened up in so many ways! I was humbled, excited, prayerful, and a bit more courageous.

The point is, after obeying Jesus, my eyes opened in new ways. So many of us want to understand something before jumping in. Not everything can be grasped from the outside. Jesus calls us into a deeper place through obedience. The coolest part of obeying Jesus' call to evangelism? I shared new stories with my students every day. Before long, they asked for gospel tracts to hand out, as well. They then started to share stories of evangelizing with others, and Christianity was a whole new ball game for them.

God desires to bless us through obedience. Not every attempt of obeying will result with glowing testimonies. Nevertheless, there are blessings for those who persevere through obedience. When giving us commands, God always has our best in mind.

Put It to Practice!

Here are a few areas of obedience that God wants to bless us through:

Serving. Volunteering does something not only for the one being helped, but also for the one helping. When you serve another person, you do something you were created to do. I have seen depressed people get better by serving others. As much as people want to be served and be comfortable, God designed us to serve others.

Encouraging. This is covered in the chapter on Communal Affirmation, but worth mentioning again. Once again, people need your encouragement and you need to learn to encourage others. Encouragement is about lifting one's spirits. People are looking for encouragement. May they find some in you!

Honoring. We are told to honor others above ourselves (Romans 12:10). Honor is an extension of encouragement.

Encouragement usually involves words. Honor also includes actions. To honor others, we need to value them as God values them. God loved the person next to you so much, He sent Jesus to die on his or her behalf! We need to honor people above, besides, and below us. God calls us to honor others, again, because He loves us.

Fasting. Nowadays, there are many facts about how fasting detoxes your body. Every major religion values fasting. When God told us to fast, it was not with the intent of making us suffer, nor was it a way of getting us to earn anything from Him. He has commanded us to fast for our own good. While the professionals in the health field can give facts on the physical benefits of fasting, there are far more benefits than they mention. The biggest includes greater clarity and a greater hunger for God. This helps hearing Him and receiving from Him to a greater degree.

Forgiving. Obedience just keeps getting more difficult, doesn't it? Well, if we've learned to practice these from an early age, it would be easier. Forgiveness is a command, according to Jesus. God desires for us to demonstrate how we have been forgiven of an astronomical debt by forgiving others of their offenses. Forgiveness is also a key in receiving God's supernatural peace.

Missions. Jesus commanded us to evangelize and to disciple all nations (Matthew 28:18-20). This is also for our good. On one hand, Jesus wants to save the lost. On the other hand, He wants us to grow in obedience, dependence, evangelizing, and discipling. If there are opportunities to go on mission trips in your church, you may be in for a surprise on the field. You can learn more in a week on the field than a year from the books.

Go throughout the Bible and take note of the different commands God gives. Instead of trying to pass over them or sweep them under the rug of "that was back then," try obeying Him believing He has great blessings for you in mind.

> *God is God. Because He is God, He is worthy of my trust and obedience. I will find rest nowhere but in His holy will, a will that is unspeakably beyond my largest notions of what He is up to.*
> **Elisabeth Elliot**[6]

---

[6] Elisabeth Elliot, *Through Gates of Splendor,* Fortieth-Anniversary Edition (Doubleday Direct, 1996), xii.

Chapter 6
Sword Training

Your word is a lamp to my feet and a light to my path.

Psalm **119:105**

Blessed is the man who walks not in the counsel of the wicked, nor stands in the way of sinners, nor sits in the seat of scoffers; but his delight is in the law of the LORD, and on his law he meditates day and night. He is like a tree planted by streams of water that yields its fruit in its season, and its leaf does not wither. In all that he does, he prospers.

Psalm 1:1-3

Do your best to present yourself to God as one approved, a worker who has no need to be ashamed, rightly handling the word of truth.

2 Timothy 2:15

Many people work out to be healthy. Some work out so they can eat whatever they want! It is difficult to be healthy without working out and watching what you eat. The same goes for your spiritual health. If you serve God and obey, but do not mind what you "eat" spiritually, you will grow unhealthy.

I am not one of those who say to never watch rated-R movies or to never listen to songs with cuss words. People can watch and listen to almost anything, as long as, they are careful to not let it change them for worse. Of course, this requires self-control and discernment.

You may have heard of the child who asked his dad if he could watch a movie with his friends that was only 5 percent bad. The father baked cookies and then put little pieces of dog poop on the cookies as replacements for chocolate chips. The father told the son to eat it because it is only 5 percent bad. The child did not eat it. Instead, he got the point and did not watch the movie either.

There is a problem with that story: Not everything the boy's father said was always good either. Not everything the boy's teachers or pastors said was 100 percent good either. Is the son to refrain from listening to such people for the rest of his life? After all, never would he eat cookies that were 5 percent bad, right? I think we get the point. The point is not to keep away from everything that is 5 percent bad (this is impossible), but rather to learn to be discerning with the "bad" that we are surrounded with.

"Bad" influences will come, whether we try or not. They are all around us.

The good, however, must be sought after.

So, what is good?

The Word of God is Good

The Word of God is good. To grow spiritually, there is no avoiding time with God in His Word. Many feel the Word is outdated and, therefore, value it less. However, the amount of years and tears it took for the Word of God to get to us should help us appreciate it more. Allow me to illustrate.

I remember serving as a traffic volunteer for a church summer school program. I would watch parents pull along the side and notify their teachers to send their children up. Wanting to be a good volunteer, I tried to engage in small encouraging talks with the parents as we waited for their children to come out. Some talks went well, others did not feel so good.

There was one particular parent, who had an adopted child. She always looked grumpy. I tried speaking to her and felt she was always angry as she smoked her cigarette and answered very concisely. I tried smiling and encouraging the mom about how her son was getting along well in the program. However, I never felt she was receptive.

Months after the program, our church had this skit presentation night. It was a big night with many skit presentations, where a lot of family and friends came to enjoy. At the end of the night as a thousand people were leaving the auditorium, greeting their friends, and figuring out what to do next, someone I didn't really talk to found her way to talk to me.

Jane said she actually had a message from me that was passed to her from somebody else (possibly two other people). I was surprised and very curious. She asked if I remember a certain student's mom from the summer school program. I did. Jane said the mom was looking for me to thank me for being very encouraging to her during that summer school time. I was taken aback for a couple of reasons. One, this mother who I thought was angry and unreceptive to me was actually thankful for me. And two, this message was passed through two or three people to get to me.

To a far greater degree, God has a greater message for us and this message has gone through hundreds of thousands of people to get to us! Oh, how we need to cherish His Word!

Reading, Studying, and Meditating

There is a difference between reading, studying, and meditating on the Word. All three are important.

Reading. Reading is simply getting through the Bible. Reading is important because it gives us the big picture. Many times we can be stuck on one particular place in the Bible. While every part of the Bible is good, not every part is complete in and of itself. It is, therefore, important to see the big picture by reading through the Bible. Learning the meaning of every chapter and verse is not the focus here. As we read, we will catch blessings and move on. Reading does not need to involve outside sources. Just you and the Bible.

Another blessing of reading the Bible is to "hear" the tone of God. Reading large portions of the Bible will help you identify God's voice and authority. Even soldiers sent to capture Jesus were amazed by the words Jesus spoke (John 7:46).

Studying. Studying is more intentional on learning about specific topics. For example, you can study a particular book, character, or theme. Studying usually involves outside sources. When studying a book of the Bible, it is important to find out the author, audience, basic content, and author's intent. When studying a character, it is important to study the development of the character. It is also important to understand, besides Jesus, no one is perfect. Characters that are praised and pointed out as examples should point us more to Christ. When studying a theme, it is important to see the theme throughout the Bible and not in just one or two isolated passages. Studying the Bible helps "put pieces together." While studying is advantageous and necessary, true studying should lead to worship. The Pharisees studied more than anyone in their time, however many of their studies led to pride. If our studies lead to pride, the answer is not to stop studying. The answer is to repent and ask God to transform our hearts.

Meditating. Meditating on the Word is about marinating in a verse or passage. To meditate means "to mutter." When we meditate on John 3:16 for example, we "mutter" the words to ourselves. We think about how much God loved us. We think about how much we sinned. We think about how much He loved Jesus. We reflect on God loving us so much that He sent Jesus to die on our behalf. We let that truth soak in. *I am loved.* Actually, *I am SO loved.* Meditating can be complemented by journaling. Writing out a verse in a chapter that blesses you and then writing your thoughts about that verse helps clarify your thoughts. After doing this for some time, you will form a collection of reflections on the Word. You will amaze yourself by your observations and insights.

There is overlap among the three. As you study, you may end up meditating on a verse or two. As you meditate on a verse, you may catch insights that you would have gained by studying it. Generally, reading the Word helps us see the big picture. Studying the Word adds depth to parts of that picture. Meditating feeds the soul.

Put It to Practice!

Ideally, reading the Bible will always be enjoyable like a lover reading a love letter in a honeymoon state. My experiences say it is not always such an easy and enjoyable experience. Thankfully, God is good at taking us beyond an unrealistic "perpetual honeymoon" to a more mature loving relationship.

Here are a few tips to help with potential bumps along the way:

For Bible Reading:

1. Set a date to complete the Bible and shoot for it! The Bible has roughly 1,200 chapters (1,189 to be exact). This means reading forty chapters a day will get you through the Bible in thirty days. Reading twenty chapters a day will get you through the Bible in sixty days. Reading ten chapters a day will get you through the Bible in 120 days. Reading five chapters a day will get you through the Bible in 240 days. Reading four chapters a day will get you through the Bible in 300 days. Calculate and go for it!

2. Knowing the rough patches helps. I have noticed three major rough patches in Bible reading: Leviticus and Deuteronomy; 1 Chronicles-2 Chronicles; and Isaiah-Daniel. These parts can be really difficult, but there is light at the end of the tunnel. Mentally preparing for these can really help. Have strength, chapters will not be added to those portions! Day by day, you can (and will) make progress. Share with people and ask them for prayer to persevere!

3. If you miss a day, DO NOT feel pressured or burdened to read double the next day! If you missed a day or two (or three), do not feel you need to read three times more to "catch up." That is not a burden from God. It's okay. Move on!

4. When you are done, congratulations! Take time to write a journal entry. What are a few main lessons you've learned from this run through the Bible? Write it down and share your blessings with someone!

For Studying:

1. Familiarize yourself with authors that can help in different topics. There are a plethora of resources online from commentaries to sermon manuscripts from Genesis to Revelation.[7]
2. Whichever study you do, enjoy it! Studying can be dry and boring. Find authors and resources that speak to you. Feel free to ask your pastors or church leaders for resources that have helped them. This may help you understand your church leaders more.
3. You know you learned something when you are able to teach it. Can you put the lessons you've learned in your own words? Practice by sharing with others what you have learned.

For Meditating:

1. Having an open Bible near you at home helps you read it.

2. Write out a verse that speaks to you. Email someone who doesn't mind receiving your reflections. Journal your thoughts concerning the verse(s). When something

---

[7] See Appendix A for more resources.

resonates, share with someone! Sharing helps further process your meditations.

3. There is no limit to how much you can meditate on a verse.

> *The Bible is not an end in itself, but a means to bring men to an intimate and satisfying knowledge of God, that they may enter into Him, that they may delight in His Presence, may taste and know the inner sweetness of the very God Himself in the core and center of their hearts.*
>
> **A.W. Tozer**[8]

---

[8] A.W. Tozer, *The Pursuit of God,* (Millennium Publications, 2014), 5.

Chapter 7
Power of Your Testimony

And they have conquered [Satan] by the blood of the Lamb and by the word of their testimony, for they loved not their lives even unto death.
Revelation 12:11

I have not hidden your deliverance within my heart;
I have spoken of your faithfulness and your salvation;
I have not concealed your steadfast love and your faithfulness from the great congregation.
Psalm 40:10

I will remember the deeds of the Lord;
yes, I will remember your wonders of old.
Psalm 77:11

Infomercials are here to stay. Whether they sell kitchen products, electronics, or exercise machines, people will buy these products. Infomercials, generally, point out a problem people can relate to, the negative consequences of the problem, and a solution (which they want you to buy, of course). To make the solution come to life, they add personal testimonies. For some reason, testimonies have a different type of authority and influence. People who give testimonies do not know the details of how to make the product, but they testify to the product's effectiveness and reliability.

Nowadays, with so many opportunities to check reviews for restaurants, products, and even professors, diligent customers will pay attention to what others have to say. Testimonies are powerful when it comes to sales, but they are also powerful in Christianity. Hearing people's testimonies can uplift your spirit in God. Sharing testimonies also helps you build more confidence. We need to speak up. For instance, friends and family can be encouraged by seeing God move in you. Pastors and leaders can also be encouraged, especially, if they have been praying for you. Now, let's check out the significance of testimonies.

5 Benefits of Christian Testimonies

1. *Testimonies are powerful!* Just as a customer's testimony can have a different level of authority than even the creator of the product, Christian testimonies have a similar effect. There was a blind man who was healed by Jesus in John 9 and testified how Jesus put mud on his eyes and told him to go wash it off in a pool. The man came back seeing and then testified before people, saying, "I washed, and I see" (v15). He once was blind, now he sees. Few could argue with his testimony. He had authority!

2. *Testimonies are personal!* When someone recalls what God did in their lives, this is more than a theory. It's one thing to hear of God's faithfulness in the pulpit or

even from the lives of people in the Bible. However, when someone speaks of God's faithfulness in their own lives, there is something personal and intimate about it.

3. *Testimonies are eternal!* People cannot take away your testimony. If you were once blind, but now you see; if you were once promiscuous, now faithful; if you were once religious, but now relational; praise God for His work in your life! No one can take that away from you! No one can take away from me how God sovereignly orchestrated for me to join the youth group where I would give my life to Christ again. No one can take away how God helped me overcome certain addictions!

4. *Testimonies are inspirational!* When people hear how God reached out to and changed a life, they can be encouraged! When people hear how God delivered someone from a bondage or dire situation they may be experiencing, hope arises. When people hear how greatly someone has changed once surrendering to God, they can't help but be amazed by the power of God. Testimonies are inspirational and encouraging to others.

5. *Testimonies are evangelistic!* There have been countless accounts of people saying of someone, "I never thought this person would ever be saved." But when they become saved and share their testimonies, more lives are changed. There is a power in testimonies that are

evangelistic. The segue from the testimony to the call to receive Christ can be smooth. There is a preaching that takes place from a changed life most sermons could not replicate.

Different Types of Testimonies

You have testimonies you need to remember and share with others! You need to remember it because God will strengthen you through it. You will recount God's hand in your own life and be encouraged in ways mere Bible truths cannot convey. And you need to share your testimony with others because they will be strengthened by it, as well. Below are different types of testimonies to have on hand.

Conversion. How did God introduce Himself to you? What was your initial response? When did you decide to give Him your all? This is one of the most important stories you'll do well to recount and have fresh in your mind. Do you know how many have been introduced to God, but cannot believe Him? For some reason, you do believe Him! This is a miracle that needs to be shared. How old were you? What was the setting? Who were the key people involved? What were you going through at that time? Was it sudden or gradual? Did you have internal conflicts or objections? After converting, what has been a few key differences in your life? Are there differences others have noticed? What are they? Also, it is perfectly fine if it was gradual and difficult to pinpoint a certain time and place. This will encourage many, as well!

Breakthroughs. Besides conversion, you must have seen God help you overcome certain sinful tendencies. What are they? Whatever they are, they can encourage others going through similar temptations. Did the victories come suddenly or gradually? Was it through prayer or other physical actions? Were there friends involved? What were the destructive consequences of the particular behavior? What were the positive consequences of overcoming such bondages? Sharing your victories helps to give much needed hope to others.

Provision. Have you seen God provide during times you were needing help? It may have been financial help, an opportunity, or a certain person to help you through difficult times. Count your blessings and revisit those stories! God has certainly miraculously brought you to this point! Through the journey, there must have been times you've needed God to come through. What were those particular times? Who was involved? What was lacking? How did God provide? You can benefit greatly by reflecting on God's hand in your life. Additionally, people everywhere need to hear of how God still provides today.

Answered prayers. Some of the above testimonies include answers to prayer. Have you seen God answer your prayers? Have you seen God move His hands to either open doors or close them? If I'm correct, not all of your prayers have been answered in the ways you have liked. I agree with all the people who have said, "There must be a reason for it not being answered," which is far from comforting at the time. However, praise God for the prayers He did answer!

God is always working and He is always working for our good (John 5:17; Romans 8:28). It will only benefit us to see what He is doing in our lives. When Paul says God is working for our good, the next verse explains "our good" as conforming us to Jesus. Our testimonies are about God's work in our lives. When we become more transformed to the image of Jesus, this is quite a remarkable testimony. How could a selfish sinner like me become more like Jesus? Only God can do such a supernatural work in my life.

During Christian gatherings, there may come a point where people can share the good things God is doing in our lives. Let's not shy away from sharing our testimonies. This is one way we overcome Satan—by sharing God's undeniably good works in our lives. Also, you don't have to wait until you get to Christian gatherings before you share your testimonies. Feel free to share them in other casual settings. God can use your story to introduce Himself to others. Keep your eyes open and you will surely be given opportunities to share your testimonies with others.

My Personal Testimony (Conversion)

Growing up without my parents in New York City, I learned about God through my Aunt Jeannie. We were living at my grandparents' home and my Aunt Jeannie was in college. When I was about five years old, she opened up the Good News Bible and told me about God. I remember having my eyes wide open. She brought me to church for a while until she married and moved away a couple of years later. After she moved, a church van would pick me up in the morning and I would take the NYC subway or bus back home by myself.

I was sent to church afterschool and summer school programs. We did homework and also had times of worship. I sincerely believed and tried my best. I particularly recall enjoying praise. Worship songs somehow really resonated with me.

Before long, however, I came to the conclusion that God existed but was not worth worshipping. I had a problem with the hypocrisy I witnessed in the church and believed God was too harsh with man.

From the sixth to eleventh grades, I held those thoughts. By the time I was in eleventh grade, I moved to the suburbs of New York in Long Island. It was quite different in the city. Because I couldn't just walk outside and meet friends, I was homebound most of the time. My family got concerned about my isolation and "encouraged" me to visit a church. I thought that was a completely wrong reason to go to church so I fought it. Regardless of my fight, I ended up visiting a small church nearby shortly after.

A few things happened at that church. One, I walked into a worship service singing songs that resonated with me several years back. A flood of emotions came to me as I heard people worshipping God as I once had. Two, I met wonderful peers. Interestingly, certain peers had similar family issues as I had. Several of them were not living with their parents and these same few also went to my school. Did I mention the youth group was only about 15-20 people? Coincidence? I slowly had my doubts. Three, I met a youth pastor, Reverend Jong (RJ) who was very gentle and fatherly. I brought up my objections about Christianity often, but he always responded with love and gentleness.

Within two months, at the beginning of a Friday night at church, I was picked randomly to pray for the group. Though I was asked to pray for the group, I recall praying aloud and re-committing my life to Christ! I recall saying the words "both feet in" this time around. I wasn't going to have one foot here and one foot there.

And my previously held objections? As I re-read the Bible, I saw God's love and provision more than His anger. Before, I saw a God constantly being mean to man. Now I saw mankind constantly sinning against a gracious God. I now saw God constantly reaching out to man, though it was God who was constantly offended. And concerning the hypocrites in the church, I learned how in the end, God will deal with me and God will deal with others. Everyone will give an account of how he or she lives. God will take care of the rest. This gave me comfort.

I'm not sure if this story resonates with you at all. Maybe you've had similar objections, maybe different. All I can say is, God was very patient and kind with me. He placed the right people in my life at the right times. He's used hardships and loneliness to get my attention. I decided to trust Him and life has never been the same since. It hasn't been difficulty-free, but it certainly has been well worth it.

If you are interested in committing or re-committing to this Christ, feel free to do so right now. Jesus has His arms wide open for you. If you know any Christian friends or leaders, they will gladly help with your questions. If you're looking for the missing piece to your life, today may just be your day to fill it. His name is Jesus and He loves you more than you can imagine.

Thank you and God bless!

Put It to Practice!

1. Try writing out different types of testimonies. Testimonies were not only made for you, but also to encourage and inspire others!

2. Try reaching out or making an invitation towards the end. Include your listener somehow. Offer hope, offer understanding, offer help.

3. After sharing your testimony with someone, ask them if they can share their testimony with you. They can also offer you much hope and encouragement through their testimony. Testimonies are powerful!

There is an appropriate way to use your story, not as an excuse but as a testimony to God's ability to free you from the past.

Andy Stanley[9]

---

[9] Andy Stanley, Enemies of the Heart: Breaking Free from the Four Emotions that Control You (Colorado Springs, CO: Multnomah, 2011): 66.

Chapter 8
The Unveiling

Everyone then who hears these words of mine and does them will be like a wise man who built his house on the rock. And the rain fell, and the floods came, and the winds blew and beat on that house, but it did not fall, because it had been founded on the rock.

Matthew 7:24-25

But he gives more grace. Therefore it says, "God opposes the proud but gives grace to the humble."

James 4:6

Repent therefore, and turn back, that your sins may be blotted out, that times of refreshing may come from the presence of the Lord, and that he may send the Christ appointed for you, Jesus.

Acts 3:19-20

When people take the seven practices revealed in the last seven chapters and work at them, their lives will never be the same. You can practice these one at a time or a few at a time. The point is to go from theory to application. So if the seven practices and teachings have been explained, why is this not the conclusion? And what is with the title of this chapter? There are a few truths about this book to unveil before we close out the discourse herein.

Unveiling Truth #1

The way to grow between spiritual highs has nothing to do with the spiritual high. Growing between retreats, revivals, and mission trips has everything to do with what you do in your normal, week to week, everyday lives.

The concept has nothing to do with retreats, revivals, mission trips and other Christian gatherings because they cannot really transform you. They can only awaken you. True transformation happens between spiritual highs in our everyday lives. What you do with what inspires or awakens you in those meetings is what is important. It's life after the meetings that really counts.[10]

Unveiling Truth #2

As a teacher and preacher, I've found the need to make adjustments as I teach. A certain "malware" has crept into many churchgoers and may have even crept into you. This epidemic is widespread and out to kill any potential blessings. Evidences of this epidemic are seen every Sunday in the looks and conversations of believers.

What is this malware you ask?

Pride.

---

[10] Pastor Benjamin Robinson, Senior Pastor of Living Hope graciously shared this insight with me personally.

Pride is a problem because God opposes the proud (James 4:6). Pride stifles growth. Pride does not see the need for God or His grace. Pride is self-sufficient. Pride thinks it is "okay" on its own. Pride cannot really learn from others. Others can learn from them, but not vice versa. Pride is deceptive and likes to mask itself under something else to not sound so bad.

Is it in you and how do you know?

In many churchgoers, pride has masked itself in two simple words:

"I know."

I know . . . I'm supposed to read the Bible.
I know . . . I'm loved by God.
I know . . . I'm supposed to pray.
I know . . . I'm supposed to be encouraging.
I know . . . I'm supposed to obey the Bible.
I know . . . everything the pastor taught about last Sunday.[11]

These two words have the greatest potential to cap and kill any good work from developing in your life. And if we're honest with ourselves, we have the tendency to use these words prematurely.

---

[11] Pastor Min Chung, Senior Pastor of Covenant Fellowship Church, shares this in his teachings on the topic of pride.

There are more sermons and messages available today than any time before. There are powerful, touching, eloquent, and Spirit-filled messages available to all of us at any time. It is quite possible we have heard many Bible teachings in many different forms. As a result, we may "know" of many teachings. But do we really? Does it show in our lives? Do others around us believe we really "know" these things?

Unveiling Truth #3

If you've been infected with the "I know" virus, which is really hidden pride, you need to repent. As said earlier, the virus won't make you open to love and encouragement from others and you won't have the drive to do so to others—all because *you know* in your head. If Solomon can learn from an ant (Proverb 6:6), we need to humble ourselves and acknowledge God can teach us through anyone or anything. We need to humble ourselves and admit we have so much more to learn concerning any topic or passage imaginable, regardless of how much we think we know.

Pride blinded the Pharisees and hindered them from receiving many blessings.

The same happens to those of us with pride today.

Usually, the ones who "know" so much do what they are comfortable doing, but do so little of what God actually wants them to do. There is a widespread need to repent of either what we know or what we think we know. God is not looking for people who can do well in Bible trivia, but people who will believe Him to the point of obeying Him.

If you think you "know" so much, but your life does not show it, the greatest action you can take today is to repent. Get back on God's side; you don't want Him opposing you! Humble yourself and you will receive much transforming grace (James 4:6). You are not alone. God will receive you and transform you by His amazing grace! Repentance is when we change our minds to conform to His will and, naturally, our actions will follow. Repentance ousts the malware out of our system and allows His Holy Spirit to lead us once again. And not only will our actions change, our emotions will too.

True repentance will bring us times of refreshing! (Acts 3:19-20)

Put It to Practice!

If you did not put any of the teachings in this book to practice, don't waste your precious time! Break your pattern by setting a new one through exercising spiritually.

Here are brief recaps of each of the seven teachings and applications for you to try implementing in your life:

Communal Affirmation. People need others. We need the encouragements of others and cannot expect them to just come to us. Sometimes we need to go to them and ask for their opinions.

Application: Ask a few people what they think your strengths, talents, and gifts are. Record these answers. Deposit much into your Encouragement Bank. If they ask, say it's for an exercise you are trying and feel free to share with them your thoughts about them!

Biblical Affirmation. People can err so it is great to have the Bible affirm us, as well. We need to have Scripture handy to know who we are, according to the Author of our lives.

Application: Share in your own words what certain Bible references say about you. Feel free to record them as you search the Scriptures. For now, here are the ten Bible references from my Biblical Encouragement Bank I've used to shape my understanding of myself:

Genesis 1:27; John 3:16; Galatians 3:26; Romans 8:17; Jeremiah 29:11; 1 Peter 4:10; Ephesians 2:10; Matthew 5:13, 14; 1 Corinthians 12:27; Romans 8:29; and John 14:12.

Self-Affirmation. There are some things people do not know about you. The Bible does not outright say certain things about you or your situation, as well. It is important to encourage yourself and preach to yourself sometimes. According to you (without contradicting the Bible), who are you really and what is really going on in your life?

Application: Take some time to counter unbiblical thoughts in your mind about you and your situation. With your understanding of God and the Bible, what is really going on in your life? What character traits is God fine-tuning in your life? Speak with authority and don't keep it in your head. Write it out!

Synergistic Prayer. Personal times of prayer are essential and necessary. However, some breakthroughs only come when praying with others. Are you willing to get uncomfortable to ask someone to pray for you on the spot? Can you bless someone with the opportunity to exercise their faith to help you break through certain difficulties? Your life will be better for it!

Application: Approach someone in person or over the phone, if necessary, and ask him or her to pray for you out loud in your presence. God will be pleased to see brothers and sisters praying for each other!

Sword Training. As food is essential to our physical health, the Word of God is essential to our spiritual health. We can gain much when we read through, study carefully, or meditate on a particular passage of the Bible.

Application: To read through the Bible, make a plan to read through a portion of the Bible (a specific book, Testament, or the entire Bible) and take that first step. Seek accountability or let others know of your plans. To study the Bible, state the book, character, or theme you would like to study. Seek out the necessary resources to study more on the topic. Start studying and increasing your knowledge on the subject. To meditate on the Bible, read the Bible until something strikes you. If you do not know where to start, start with the Proverbs. When you read something that speaks to you, stay there. Write out your reflections on that particular passage. What word or words stand out to you? How does this help your view of God or self? Repeat this process. Believe it or not, you can find strength all throughout the Bible.

Personal Testimony. Remembering what God has done in your life is not to be understated. God has been working in your life before you were born. Blessed are you when you recognize God's hand in your life. You will gain strength when you notice God working on your behalf.

Application: How did you come to believe and surrender to Jesus? How old were you? What were you going through? Who were the key player(s)? What breakthroughs have you accomplished because of the Lord? What were you like before the breakthrough and what were you like after? How has God come through in crucial times for you? Recount God working in your life. You need to identify your blessings before you can count them! Write it out and look for times to share with someone.

Has the Word of God really gone into your heart? May it manifest through your actions!

Knowing what you should do and actually doing what you should do is the difference between growing and dying. Growing through spiritual highs requires action between spiritual highs.

Satan doesn't mind Bible study never put into practice.
Rick Warren[12]

---

[12] Rick Warren, "Satan Doesn't Mind Bible Study Never Put Into Practice," Pastor Rick's Daily Hope. http://pastorrick.com/devotional/english/satan-doesn-t-mind-bible-study-never-put-into-practice (Accessed May 19, 2017).

Conclusion

One time, I became so sick of these constant ups and downs, I told God, "I will no longer go up and down. From now on, I will always be . . . down!" I tried to run away, but within half an hour of that declaration, I felt unbearable stomach pain out of nowhere! I repented quickly. Since always being down was not an option, I tried to learn how to keep my tank full. That's what I learned as a big part of the journey: learning how to keep your tank full.

As a pastor, I hurt when I see people depending too much on the church to fulfill all their needs. Most churches, I understand, do try to be faithful to their congregation. However, few churches (if any) have what it takes to completely fulfill their members. Part of the process of growing is taking initiative to position yourself to receive more of God's grace.

God does not desire anyone to constantly go up and down all throughout their lives. He does not desire anyone to be tossed back and forth like the waves. He desires His children to be steady and filled. The applied teachings in this book have been time tested and approved. Once again, notice I did not say these "teachings," but rather these "applied teachings."

Sometimes we need to do what may not feel natural to us to experience supernatural results.

I want to leave you with this: you are not alone in this journey.

Heaven is cheering for you (Hebrews 12:1).

Our spiritual brothers and sisters are rooting for us to grow to new levels.

The more we grow, the greater contributions we will make to others.

God is on our side and the ball is on our court!

It's going to take some practice, but it will well be worth it.

Spiritual highs from mission trips and conferences are wonderful.

But remember: true success does not come during our spiritual highs, they come between our spiritual highs.

Postscript

I can hardly believe what just happened! I'm just a half time associate pastor at my church. I completed my M.Div. from an online seminary a few months ago and just published a book someone was willing to read all the way through. With the self-doubts that I have had on and off for many years, I guess this book you hold (or read on your device) is evidence of these practices being practiced in my own life.

Before we part for the time being, I would like to bless you with some encouragements and affirmations for your interest on this topic and help you go further.

Final Exhortations

Brother or Sister in Christ,

God has fearfully and wonderfully made you (Psalm 139:14).

God has determined the times and places you would live in (Acts 17:26).

God has loved you with an everlasting love (Jeremiah 31:3).

God has called you to repent of your sins and to follow Him (Matthew 4:17).

God and His heavenly angels rejoiced in heaven when you repented (Luke 15:10, 20).

You are called to love God and to love others with His supernatural love (Matthew 22:37-39).

You are called to be His light and to shine His ways (Matthew 5:14).

You are called for specific good works only you can do (Ephesians 2:10).

You are commissioned to make a difference by evangelizing and making disciples of all nations (Matthew 28:18-20).

You are not left alone (Hebrews 13:5).

God is with you in your highest of highs and your lowest of lows (Psalm 139:8).

He has given you leaders to equip you (Ephesians 4:11-12).

He has given you a body of believers to work with (1 Corinthians 12:12-27).

He has given you the Word of God to train you up in righteousness (2 Timothy 3:16).

God desires to accomplish His good purposes through you (Philippians 2:13).

And He will finish the good work He began in you (Philippians 1:6).

So be of good cheer, Jesus has overcome the world! (John 16:33)

Trust God with the gifts and talents He has given you! (Matthew 25:14-15)

Continue to do good and expect to reap a harvest in due time! (Galatians 6:9)

Be strong and courageous for the LORD your God will be with you wherever you go! (Joshua 1:9)

Local and Global Impact

As a pastor, I desire not only to "give fish," but more so to "teach how to fish." To be more accurate, I desire to teach others how to teach others "how to fish" so forth and so on.

Actually as believers, we are all called to evangelize and make disciples of all nations (Matthew 28:18-20). We are called to make an impact for Christ locally and globally (Acts 1:8). This will be a lifetime process. For myself, this book is one of many attempts to accomplish this.

So what is your attempt?

You and I have been given the baton to bless and train others to impact the world. We may do it in different ways, but we have to do it. If you are alive and your heart is still beating, God isn't finished with you yet! You are called to greatness. The world is waiting for you and I to wake up to who we truly are in Christ (Romans 8:19). The world is waiting for us to truly show them the supernatural love and ways of God.

In my ongoing journey, I commit to serving the local and global church. I commit to stepping up my game in making an impact locally and globally for the rest of my life.

What about you?

If you would like to possibly partner together on making an impact for Christ locally and globally or would like to share how God has moved you through this book in any way, please email me at: betweenspiritualhighs@gmail.com.

I pray for spiritual highs in your life, but more importantly, a blessed lifestyle between your spiritual highs—one that will impact nations and generations!

Appendix A

Bible

Anders, Max. *30 Days to understanding the Bible.* Nashville, TN: Thomas Nelson, 2004.

Fee, Gordon D. and Douglas Stuart. *How to Read the Bible for All Its Worth.* 4th Edition. Grand Rapids, MI: Zondervan, 2014.

Fee, Gordon D., and Douglas Stuart. *How to Read the Bible Book by Book: A Guided Tour.* Zondervan, 2009.

Commentaries

Henry, Matthew. Matthew Henry's Commentary on the Whole Bible: Complete and Unabridged. Peabody, MA: Hendrickson Publishers, 1991.

J. Vernon McGee's "Thru the Bible" Commentary Series.

Warren Wiersbe's "Be" Series.

Bible Characters

"Great Lives" Series by Charles Swindoll (Including: David, Esther, Joseph, Moses, Elijah, Paul, Job, and Jesus)

Theology

Pink, A.W. The Attributes of God. Grand Rapids, MI: Baker Books, 1975.

Packer, J.I. Knowing God. Downers Grove, IL: Intervarsity Press, 1973.

Spiritual Gifts

Deere, Jack. Surprised by the Voice of God. Grand Rapids, MI: Zondervan, 1996.

Deere, Jack. Surprised by the Power of the Spirit. Grand Rapids, MI: Zondervan, 1993.

Clark, Randy. There Is More!: The Secret to Experiencing God's Power to Change Your Life. Minneapolis, MN: Chosen Books, 2013.

Prayer

Bounds, E. M. E.M. Bounds on Prayer. New Kensington, PA: Whitaker House, 1997.

Wilkinson, Bruce. Prayer of Jabez: Breaking Through to the Blessed Life. Sisters, OR: Multnomah Publishers, Inc., 2000.

Cymbala Jim and Dean Merrill. Fresh Wind, Fresh Fire: What Happens When God's Spirit Invades the Hearts of His People. Grand Rapids, MI: Zondervan, 1997.

Murray, Andrew. With Christ in the School of Prayer. Okitoks Press, 2017.

Sheets, Dutch. Intercessory Prayer: How God Can Use Your Prayers to Move Heaven and Earth. Bloomington, MN: Bethany House Publishers, 1996.

Fasting

Towns, Elmer. Fasting for Spiritual Breakthrough: A Guide to Nine Biblical Fasts. Bloomington, MN: Bethany House Publishers, 2010.

Brooks, Steven. Fasting and Prayer: God's Nuclear Power. Shippensburg, PA: Destiny Image, 2012.

Evangelism

Earley, Dave and David Wheeler. Evangelism Is: How to Share Jesus with Passion and Confidence. Nashville, TN: B&H Publishing, 2010.

Cahill, Mark. One Heartbeat Away: Your Journey into Eternity. 5th edition. Rockwall, Tex.: Mark Cahill Ministries, 2005.

Discipleship

Earley, Dave and Rod Dempsey. Disciple Making Is: How to Live the Great Commission with Passion and Confidence. Nashville, TN: B&H Publishing, 2013.

Gallaty, Robby. Rediscovering Discipleship: Making Jesus' Final Words Our First Work. Grand Rapids, Michigan: Zondervan, 2015.

Cole, Neil. Cultivating a Life for God: Multiplying Disciples through Life Transformation Groups. CMA Resources, 2014.

Leadership

Blackaby, Henry, and Richard Blackaby. Spiritual Leadership: Moving People on to God's Agenda. Revised and Updated Edition. Nashville, TN: Thomas Nelson, 2011.

Sanders, J. Oswald. Spiritual Leadership: Principles of Excellence for Every Believer. Second Revision. Chicago, IL: Moody Bible Institute, 2007.

Hybels, Bill. Courageous Leadership: Field-Tested Strategy for the 360 Leader. Reprint edition. Grand Rapids, MI: Zondervan, 2012.

Money/Giving

Alcorn, Randy. Money, Possessions, and Eternity. Revised and Updated Edition. Carol Stream, IL: Tyndale House Publishers, Inc., 2003.

Lupton, Robert D. Toxic Charity: How Churches and Charities Hurt Those They Help, And How to Reverse It. 1 edition. New York, NY: HarperOne, 2012.

Identity

Driscoll, Mark. Who Do You Think You Are?: Finding Your True Identity in Christ. 1st Edition. Nashville, TN: Thomas Nelson, 2013.

Vallotton, Kris, and Bill Johnson. The Supernatural Ways of Royalty: Discovering Your Rights and Privileges of Being a Son or Daughter of God. 1st edition. Shippensburg, PA: Destiny Image Publishers, 2006.

Revival

Engle, Lou, Catherine Paine, and Tommy Tenney. Digging the Wells of Revival: Reclaiming Your Historic Inheritance Through Prophetic Intercession. Shippensburg, PA: Destiny Image Publishers, 1998.

Hansen, Collin, and John D. Woodbridge. A God-Sized Vision: Revival Stories That Stretch and Stir. Grand Rapids, MI: Zondervan, 2015.

Manhood

Eldredge, John. Fathered By God: Learning What Your Dad Could Never Teach You. Nashville, TN: Thomas Nelson, 2009.

Eldredge, John. Wild at Heart Revised and Updated: Discovering the Secret of a Man's Soul. Revised and Updated edition. Nashville, NT: Thomas Nelson, 2011.

Womanhood

Bevere, Lisa. Girls with Swords: How to Carry Your Cross Like a Hero. Colorado Springs, CO: Waterbrook Press, 2013.

Bevere, Lisa. Lioness Arising: Wake Up and Change Your World. Colorado Springs, CO: Waterbrook Press, 2010.

Eldredge, John, and Stasi Eldredge. Captivating Revised and Updated: Unveiling the Mystery of a Woman's Soul. Nashville, TN: Thomas Nelson, 2011.

Church

Rainer, Thom S, and Eric Geiger. Simple Church: Returning to God's Process for Making Disciples. Nashville, TN: B&H Publishing, 2011.

Warren, Rick. The Purpose Driven Church: Every Church is Big in God's Eyes. Grand Rapids, MI: Zondervan, 1995.

Cole, Neil. Organic Church: Growing Faith Where Life Happens. 1 edition. San Francisco, CA: Jossey-Bass, 2005.

Apologetics

Lewis, C. S., and Kathleen Norris. Mere Christianity. Revised & Enlarged edition. San Francisco: HarperOne, 2015.

Strobel, Lee. The Case for Christ: A Journalist's Personal Investigation of the Evidence for Jesus. Grand Rapids, MI: Zondervan, 1998.

Strobel, Lee. The Case for Faith: A Journalist Investigates the Toughest Objections to Christianity. Grand Rapids, MI: Zondervan, 2000.

Christian Living

Murray, Andrew. An Exciting New Life. Springdale, Pa.: Whitaker House, 1996.

Silk, Danny. Keep Your Love On: Connection, Communication & Boundaries. Redding, CA: Red Arrow Media, 2013.

Bevere, John. Under Cover: The Promise of Protection Under His Authority. Nashville, TN: Thomas Nelson, 2001.

Bevere, John. The Bait of Satan: Living Free From the Deadly Trap of Offense. Revised edition. Lake Mary, FL: Charisma House, 2004.

Warren, Richard. The Purpose-Driven Life: What on Earth Am I Here for? Grand Rapids, Mich: Zondervan, 2002.

About the Author

Sunny Kang has regularly been a part of, led, and spoken at many youth events in America and oversees. He has pastored in children's, youth, college, and young adult ministries. He also speaks regularly to the homeless, addicted, and others in need. Sunny has a vision of planting multi-cultural and multi-ethnic churches, beginning in Las Vegas one day. He and his wife, Anna, live and serve in Las Vegas.